Guided Reading Notes

Purple Band
Oxford Level 8

Water

Contents

OXFORD
UNIVERSITY PRESS

Introduction

Why is guided reading important?

Guided reading plays an important role in your whole-school provision for reading, providing opportunities for children to progress and develop the key competencies they need to become confident and skilled independent readers. Working with small groups of children, with texts closely matched to the readers' needs, guided reading is the perfect vehicle for delivering focused teaching from Reception/P1 right through to Year 6/P7. The teacher-pupil interaction also provides a valuable assessment opportunity, helping you identify exactly what each child can and can't do. Through guided reading children also encounter a world of exciting, whole books – building a community of readers who read for pleasure.

About *Project X Origins*

Project X Origins is a comprehensive, whole-school guided reading programme designed to help you teach the wide range of skills essential to ensure children progress as readers and to help nurture a love of reading.

Ensuring the key skills are covered

Project X Origins incorporates all of the key skills children need to develop to become successful and enthusiastic readers:

> **Word reading:** phonically regular and common exception words are introduced systematically in the early levels with phonic opportunities provided throughout the notes. As children progress, they are encouraged to use their decoding skills whenever they encounter new or unfamiliar words, and also to recognize how this impacts on different spelling rules.

> **Comprehension:** understanding what has been read is central to being an effective and engaged reader but comprehension is not something that comes automatically so specific strategies have been built into the notes to ensure children develop comprehension skills they can use over a range of texts:

- Previewing
- Predicting
- Activating and building prior knowledge
- Questioning
- Recalling
- Visualizing and other sensory responses
- Deducing, inferring and drawing conclusions
- Determining importance
- Synthesizing
- Empathizing
- Summarizing
- Personal response, including adopting a critical response

> **Reading fluency:** fluency occurs as children develop automatic word recognition, reading with pace and expression. Strategies to help achieve this, including meaningful opportunities for oral reading, re-reading and re-listening are provided throughout.

> **Vocabulary:** introducing new vocabulary within a meaningful context is an important element in extending children's vocabulary range, developing their reading fluency and comprehension. Each thematic cluster provides opportunities for revisiting and reinforcing vocabulary over a range of books and contexts.

> **Grammar, punctuation and spelling:** learning about language in the context of a text, rather than through a series of discrete exercises, can help make grammar, punctuation and spelling relevant and helps children make the link between grammar, punctuation and clarity of meaning, thus supporting their development as writers. Opportunities to support an in-depth look at language are provided for every book from Year I/P2 to Year 6/P7.

> **Spoken language:** talk is crucial to learning and developing their comprehension so children are given plenty of opportunities to: discuss and debate their ideas with others; justify their opinions; ask and answer questions; explore and hypothesise; summarise, describe and explain; and listen and respond to the ideas of others.

Assessment and progression in reading

Project X Origins includes a rigorous assessment spine drawn from the *Oxford Reading Criterion Scale* to ensure that you know exactly what each child can do and what they need to focus on next in order to make progress. This assessment framework, combined with the careful levelling of the Oxford Levels, will help you select the right book with the right level of challenge for each of your guided reading groups and to assess, track and monitor each child's progress.

⟩ Step 1

On a termly basis, use the *Oxford Reading Criterion Scale* (which can be found in the relevant *Project X Origins Teaching Handbook*) to assess each child's reading. The scale will tell you the Oxford Level a child is comfortable reading at, and the areas a child needs to develop. You can also use this assessment to form your guided reading groups.

⟩ Step 2

Plan your guided reading sessions by selecting books at the appropriate Oxford Level that focus on the relevant learning needs of the group. You will find charts showing the learning objectives and assessment points for every *Project X Origins* book in the relevant *Project X Origins Teaching Handbook*. Depending on your assessment, you might choose a book at the level the children are comfortable at or one from the next level up, to offer some stretch.

⟩ Step 3

Use the assessment points within the Guided Reading Notes to support on-going assessment of children's reading progress. The Progress Tracking Charts in the relevant *Project X Origins Teaching Handbook* can be used to record this if you wish. Regularly re-assess each child's progress combining your on-going informal assessments and the termly assessment using the *Oxford Reading Criterion Scale*. Use this information to re-organize guided reading groups and teaching plans in response to children's varying degrees of progress.

Getting started: using the Guided Reading Notes

At a glance
Project X Origins Guided Reading Notes offer detailed guidance to help deliver effective and engaging guided reading sessions, and are designed to be used flexibly to ensure you get the most out of each book. For notes containing multiple sessions, you may choose to focus on each of these sessions or focus on one session and have the children read the rest of the book independently.

Curricular correlation and assessment
At the beginning of every set of notes there are correlation charts for all UK curricula, ensuring that across the clusters the main curricular objectives are covered. In addition, an overview of assessment points for each book is provided – these points are also signposted throughout the notes.

Key information
Before the first session, an overview of the book and the resources you will need (such as additional photocopy masters) is provided.

Teaching sequence
Each guided reading session follows the same teaching sequence:

- **Before reading**: children explore the context of each book to support their understanding and help them engage with the text. They are encouraged to discuss, recall, respond, predict and speculate about the book. Opportunities to focus on word reading and/or vocabulary are also introduced at this point.
- **During reading**: children are given a section of the book to read with specific questions in mind.
- **After reading**: children reflect on and discuss what they have read. They are encouraged to delve deeper, exploring their understanding of the text, developing their vocabulary, grammar, punctuation, spelling and fluency where appropriate.
- **Follow-up**: opportunities for children to extend their learning outside the session are provided, including writing and cross-curricular activities.

Throughout the sessions, the key strategies that children are developing are clearly identified.

A Wild Ride

BY TONY BRADMAN

Curricular correlation

English National Curriculum

Spoken language	Participate in discussions and debates
Word reading	Read accurately by blending the sounds in words that contain the graphemes taught so far, especially recognising alternative sounds for graphemes
Comprehension	Discuss their favourite words and phrases
	Participate in discussion about books, taking turns and listening to what others say
	Predict what might happen on the basis of what has been read so far

Phonics and vocabulary

GPCs	/ee/ three, he, screamed
Decodable 2 and 3 syllable words	outside, acorn, current, skimming
Common exception words	suddenly, window, through, shouted, water, three, something
Challenge and context words	build, paddle, whoosh, whizzed, awesome, wild, scared, fence, island, phew, move, water

Developing grammar, punctuation and spelling

Grammar and Punctuation	Apostrophes to mark where letters are missing in spelling	let's, I'm, it's, what's, don't, we're, we'll, can't
Spelling	The /o/ sound spelt 'a' after 'w'	watches, want, was

Reading assessment points (Oxford Reading Criterion Scale: Assessment Standard 3)

3.	Can the children apply phonic skills and knowledge to recognize an increasing number of complex words? (READ)
6.	Can the children locate some specific information e.g. key events, characters' names etc. or key information on a non-fiction page? (R)
14.	Can the children read words with contractions (e.g. I'm, I'll, we'll, he's) and understand that the apostrophe represents the omitted letter(s)? (READ)
21.	Can the children talk about how different words and phrases affect meaning? (E)
23.	Are the children beginning to read between the lines, using clues from text and pictures, to discuss thoughts, feelings and actions? (D)

Scottish Curriculum for Excellence

Listening and talking	I can select ideas and relevant information, organise these in a logical sequence and use words which will be interesting and/or useful for others LIT I-06u
Reading	I can use my knowledge of sight vocabulary, phonics, context clues, punctuation and grammar to read with understanding and expression ENG I-12a
	I can share my thoughts about structure, characters and/or setting comment on the effective choice of words and other features ENG I-19a

Foundation Phase Framework in Wales

Oracy	Extend their ideas or accounts by sequencing what they say and including relevant details (Speaking)
Reading	Apply the following reading strategies with increasing independence to a range of familiar and unfamiliar texts: phonic strategies, recognition of high-frequency words, context clues, e.g. *prior knowledge*, graphic and syntactic clues, and self-correction, including re-reading and reading ahead (Reading strategies)
	Show understanding and express opinions about language, information and events in texts (Response and analysis)
	Look for clues in the text to understand information (Reading strategies)

Northern Ireland Curriculum

Talking and Listening	Speak audibly and clearly, using appropriate quality of speech and voice
Reading	Express opinions and give reasons based on what they have read

About this book

This is the first part in a two-part story. It's a rainy day so the friends decide to make a raft. They get more than they bargained for when they take it for a ride and the raft becomes out of control. Readers are left with a cliffhanger ending and the story continues in *Don't Look Down*.

You will need

■ *A Wild Ride board game* Photocopy Master, *Teaching Handbook* for Year 2/P3

■ *Water words* Photocopy Master, *Teaching Handbook* for Year 2/P3

> Before reading

■ Look at the cover and ask the children to guess where the characters are. What is the weather like? How can they tell? **(deducing, inferring)**

■ Look at the expressions on the faces of the characters. What do they think the characters are feeling? **(empathizing)**

■ Ask them if they have ever been on a 'wild' ride. What was it like? What sort of wild ride do they think this story will be about? **(activating prior knowledge, predicting)**

■ Discuss the sorts of activities that Max and his friends might do if it is too wet to go out and play. **(activating prior knowledge)**

■ Ask the children to look at the 'water words', e.g. *flowed*, *splashed* (p.6), *river* (p.7), *paddle* (p.8), *gushed* (p.11), *rapids* (p.13), *current* (p.16), *spray* (p.18). If necessary, help them decode the words. Discuss the meaning of the words and create a water-related word wall. The words can be written on paper leaves floating down the river, on fish swimming beneath the surface, or on water droplets from rain or a waterfall. Alternatively, you could use the *Water words* Photocopy Master. Continue to add any words that relate to the water theme as the children read this cluster of books, and encourage them to think of their own examples. **(word reading, developing vocabulary)**

■ To build up tension, model how to read pages 2–5 with expression and clarity. **(engaging readers)**

Phonic opportunity

- Draw attention to all of the words with the **/ee/** phoneme: *three*, *he*, *screamed*. Ask children to identify the phoneme /ee/ in the words. Support children to say each phoneme and then blend the phonemes to read the word. Ask children to think of other words with the /ee/ sound.

- You may wish to point out some of the common exception words, or practise decoding some of the challenge and context words in this book.

During reading

- Ask the children what they should do if they encounter a difficult word, modelling with an example from the book. Praise children who successfully decode unfamiliar words.

- Ask them to read to the end of the book.

- As they read, ask them to notice the 'water words' you have shared plus any other water-related vocabulary, e.g. *life jackets* (p.9).

Assessment point

Can the children apply phonic skills and knowledge to recognize an increasing number of complex words? (ORCS Standard 3, 3)

"We'll have to jump!" shouted Max.
The raft was now skimming across the grass. The air was filled with spray.
"On the count of three," yelled Max.
"One ... two ... THREE!"

Max, Cat and Tiger jumped clear but Ant was too scared to let go. He clung on to the raft.
"*HELP!*" cried Ant.
"I can't look," said Cat.

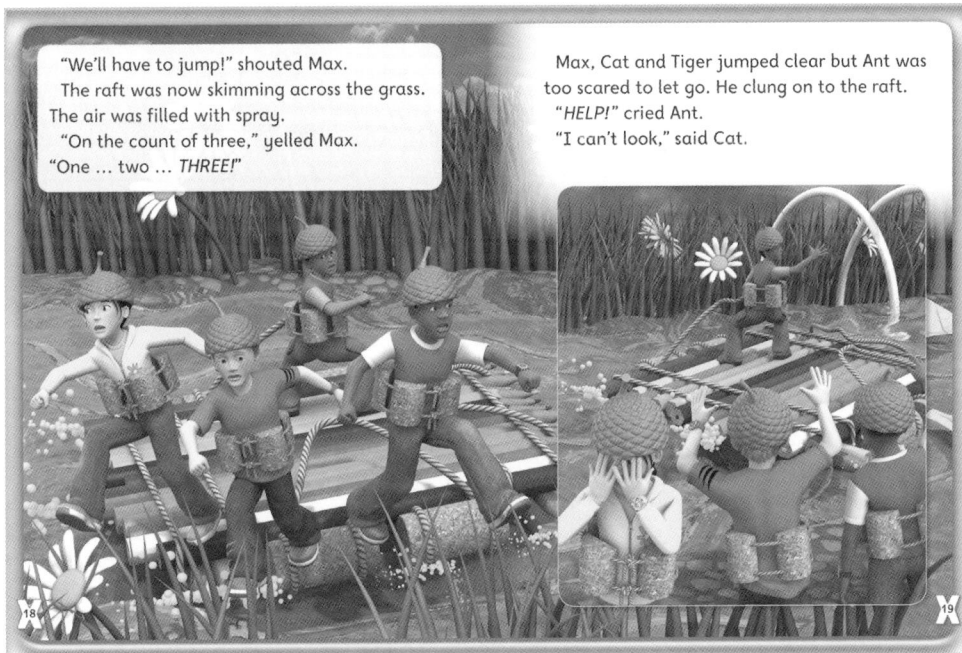

> After reading

Returning to the text

Ask the children:

- Why did the path look like a river to the micro-friends? **(activating prior knowledge, deducing, inferring)**
- Who had the idea of building their own raft? **(recalling)**
- How do you know when the friends are not enjoying themselves any more? What words do they use to express their feelings? **(inferring)**
- How do you think Ant is feeling at the end of this story? **(empathizing)** ≪ ≪ ≪
- What do you think will happen to the friends in the next book? **(predicting)**

> **Assessment point**
>
> Can the children locate some specific information e.g. key events, characters' names etc. or key information on a non-fiction page?
> (ORCS Standard 3, 6)

>> *Developing comprehension*

- Discuss the author's use of capitals for whole words, e.g. *FUN!* (p.4), *SPLASH!* (pp.14, 16), *THREE!* (p.18). Why are these words in capitals?
- Why has the author used italics on page 4 when Max says "*What's that?*" Ask the children how it affects the way they read the text. How might they use the same techniques in their own writing? ≪ ≪ ≪

> **Assessment point**
>
> Can the children talk about how different words and phrases affect meaning?
> (ORCS Standard 3, 21)

⟩ *Developing vocabulary*

- Ask the children to play the listening game 'telephone conversations' in pairs. This encourages the use of language rather than gesture. They should sit back to back with imaginary telephones for conversation. One person is Ant when he is stranded at the end of the book and the other is Cat. They should discuss how each of them is feeling and how Max, Cat and Tiger might be able to rescue Ant. **(empathizing, predicting)** ≪≪≪≪

Assessment point

Are the children beginning to read between the lines, using clues from text and pictures, to discuss thoughts, feelings and actions?
(ORCS Standard 3, 23)

⟩ *Developing grammar, punctuation and spelling*

- Look at the words containing apostrophes noted by the children and explain that apostrophes show where letters are missed out of a word (contractions), e.g. *it's*, *let's*. Explain that the apostrophe replaces a letter, so in *it's* (it is), the second 'i' is replaced by the apostrophe.
- Write the words *watches* and *was* on the board and ask children for the sound that they can hear in each. Discuss how the /o/ sound is sometimes spelt with an 'a' after 'w'. Can they ≪≪ think of any other examples?

Assessment point

Can the children read words with contractions, (e.g. I'm, I'll, we'll, he's) and understand that the apostrophe represents the omitted letter(s)?
(ORCS Standard 3, 14)

❯ Follow-up

Writing activities

- Write some basic instructions for building a raft.
  (short writing task)
- In pairs, complete and then play the *A Wild Ride board game*
  Photocopy Master based on the story. This activity is ideal for
  when it is too wet to go outside! **(short writing task)**

Cross-curricular activities

- Investigate which materials would be best to make a raft for
  children, or a life jacket, or a helmet? Which materials would
  not be suitable and why? Sort the materials into two groups.
  (Science)
- Compose a sound picture of *A Wild Ride* using tuned and
  untuned percussion instruments. Record the musical ideas
  using invented signs and symbols. Rehearse and perform the
  composition. **(Music)**
- Take digital photographs of the role-plays. Download
  the photographs into presentation software and ask the
  children to discuss what the actors were saying. They could
  add call outs as speech bubbles or compose a description
  underneath each photograph. They could also record dialogue
  to go with each slide. **(Computing)**

"Ant!" yelled Cat. "Are you OK?"
Ant got to his feet and waved.
"Phew!" said Max. "Now all we have to do is get him back."
Tiger looked around at the broken raft. "How are we going to do that, Max?" he said.

Cat looked out across the pond. Poor Ant seemed smaller than ever! Then she saw something move in the water. A giant shadow swam past.
"I think we need a bigger raft," said Cat …

To be continued …

Don't Look Down
BY TONY BRADMAN

Curricular correlation

English National Curriculum

Spoken language	Articulate and justify answers, arguments and opinions
Word reading	Read aloud books closely matched to their improving phonic knowledge, sounding out unfamiliar words accurately, automatically and without undue hesitation
Comprehension	Discuss and clarify the meanings of words, linking new meanings to known vocabulary
	Discuss the sequence of events in books and how items of information are related
	Listen to, discuss and express views about stories at a level beyond that at which they can read independently

Phonics and vocabulary

GPCs	/or/ caught, saw, your, boring
Decodable 2 and 3 syllable words	shadow, flapping, whispered, passing, splashed, landed, followed, pockets
Common exception words	something, fast, thought, where, were
Challenge and context words	water, breaks, island, eye, heard, idea, know, whispered, ocean, rustled, scientific, answer

Developing grammar, punctuation and spelling

Grammar and Punctuation	Expanded noun phrases for description and specification	huge fish, big mouth, tiny green dot, horrible fish, huge shadow
Spelling	Adding -ed to words of one syllable ending in a single consonant letter after a single vowel letter	dropped, stopped, strapped, dipped, skimmed

Reading assessment points (Oxford Reading Criterion Scale: Assessment Standard 3)

1. Can the children identify when reading does not make sense and self-correct in order for the text to make sense? (READ)
9. Can the children provide simple explanations about events or information, e.g. why a character acted in a particular way? (D)
21. Can the children talk about how different words and phrases affect meaning? (E)
23. Are children beginning to read between the lines, using clues from text and illustrations, to discuss thoughts, feelings and actions? (D)

Scottish Curriculum for Excellence

Listening and talking	I can comment on the effective choice of words and other features ENG 1-19a
Reading	I can use my knowledge of sight vocabulary, phonics, context clues, punctuation and grammar to read with understanding and expression ENG 1-12a
	I can share my thoughts about structure, characters and/or setting ENG 1-19a

Foundation Phase Framework in Wales

Oracy	Extend their ideas or accounts by sequencing what they say and including relevant details (Speaking)
Reading	Apply the following reading strategies with increasing independence to a range of familiar and unfamiliar texts: phonic strategies, recognition of high-frequency words, context clues, e.g. prior *knowledge*, graphic and syntactic clues, and self-correction, including re-reading and reading ahead (Reading strategies)
	Draw upon relevant personal experience and prior knowledge to support understanding of texts (Comprehension)

Northern Ireland Curriculum

Talking and Listening	Begin to use evidence from text to support their views
Reading	Use a range of comprehension skills, both oral and written, to interpret and discuss texts

About this book

This is the second part in a two-part story, started in *A Wild Ride*. The children's raft has been smashed to bits and Ant is stuck on an island in the middle of a pond. Max and the others have to rescue him.

You will need

- *Dragonfly Photocopy* Master, *Teaching Handbook* for Year 2/P3
- *Dragonfly life cycle* Photocopy Master, *Teaching Handbook* for Year 2/P3

❯ Before reading

- Look at the cover and ask the children if they can remember where the characters are and what the problem is. **(recall, summarizing)**

- On page 3, the author says that Max, Cat and Tiger jumped *just in time*. What might have happened if they had stayed on the raft? Have you ever done something just in time? **(empathizing)**

- Have a book about freshwater habitats ready (or take the children to the school library). Discuss the different kinds of animals, especially insects, fish and amphibians, that live in or near a pond or stream. **(previewing, engaging readers)**

- Ask the children to look at the 'water words', e.g. *stuck in the mud*, *huge drops of water*, *splashed* (p.8), *skimmed across the water* (p.13). If necessary, help children decode the words and discuss their meanings. **(developing vocabulary)**

- If you have not already set up a water-related word wall, you could do so now. Otherwise, continue to add any water-related words and phrases to the word wall. Encourage the children to think of their own examples. **(developing vocabulary)**

- Read page 4 aloud to the children, building the tension. Ask them what the author wants the reader to think has happened to Ant. They could take turns to read the page, emphasizing the suspense. How does the illustration help? **(engaging readers, predicting)** ≪≪≪≪≪≪

> Are children beginning to read between the lines, using clues from text and illustrations, to discuss thoughts, feelings and actions?
> (ORCS Standard 3, 23)

⤳ *Phonic opportunity*

- Draw attention to all of the words with the /**or**/ phoneme: *caught, saw, your, boring*. Ask the children to identify the phoneme /or/ in the words. Support children to say each phoneme and then blend the phonemes to read the word. Ask the children to think of other words with the /or/ sound.
- You may also wish to point out some of the common exception words, or practise decoding some of the challenge and context words in this book.

❭ **During reading**

- Ask the children what they should do if they encounter a difficult word, modelling with an example from the book. Praise children who successfully decode unfamiliar words. ≪≪≪≪≪≪

> **Assessment point**
> Can the children identify when reading does not make sense and self-correct in order for the text to make sense?
> (ORCS Standard 3, 1)

- Pause at the end of page 5 and ask the children to compare the expressions of the children on this page with those on page 4. How does Cat know that Ant is OK? Ask them if they know of any other devices in books or films that show where the characters are. **(deducing, inferring)**
- Ask them to read to the end of the book. As they read, invite them to notice the 'water words' and phrases you have shared plus any other water-related vocabulary.
- Ask the children to look out for words with the -ed suffix as they read and to make a mental note of interesting descriptive noun phrases.

> After reading

Returning to the text

Ask the children:

- What are people able to do now that it has stopped raining (p.7)? **(activating prior knowledge)**

- Why does *gulped* (p.13) make you think of the huge fish as well as Max? **(visualizing)**

- Make a list of the wildlife seen by Max and Ant. **(recall)**

- Look at the text and illustrations on pages 15–17. How do the author and illustrator show that Ant is having a good time when Max finds him? **(empathizing)**

- Would you like to be a micro-explorer? **(personal response)**

- Do you think that the title of this book *Don't Look Down* works well? Can you explain why? **(personal response, adopting a critical stance)**

> **Assessment point**
>
> Can the children provide simple explanations about events or information, e.g. why a character acted in a particular way? (ORCS Standard 3, 9)

> Developing comprehension

- Ask the children to play the listening game 'babble gabble' in pairs. After the initial reading, one child begins to retell the story to a partner as fast as he or she can, but with as much attention to detail as possible. After a minute, the teacher calls 'change' and the listener now has to continue with the story. This pattern continues for a number of turns. It is important to let the children know they do not have to tell the story in the same words as the book. However, they do have to listen carefully in order to remember the plot and sequence of events. **(recall)**

→ Developing vocabulary

- Point out the phrase on page 9, *fast as a flea*. Why did the author use *flea* as a comparison and *jump* to show how Max hitched a ride with the dog? (Dogs have fleas that jump.)

- Discuss the use of the phrase on page 12, *as wide as the ocean*. « « «

- Ask the children to create phrases of their own to describe the micro-copter, e.g. *as light as a feather, as fast as a jet, as colourful as a dragonfly*.

Assessment point

Can the children talk about how different words and phrases affect meaning?
(ORCS Standard 3, 21)

→ Developing grammar, punctuation and spelling

- Write the word *dot* on the board and ask the children to explain what picture they have in their heads. Now write *tiny green dot* on the board and ask them how their image has changed. Discuss how the expanded noun phrase adds detail and makes the information more specific for the reader. Challenge children to look through the book and identify other examples of expanded noun phrases that add specific details.

- Look at the words the children have collected with the *-ed* suffix. Look at the examples they've found where there is a double consonant before the *-ed*. Discuss the spelling rule: if a one-syllable verb has a short vowel sound and ends in a consonant you need to double the consonant before adding *-ed*. Explain that this rule can also be applied to adding *-ing, -er, -est* and *-y* to words that end in an 'e'.

》Follow-up

Writing activities

■ Invite the children to create a short descriptive writing piece describing in detail what it was like for Max in the mud and long, wet grass on pages 8–9. They could try to include figurative language. **(longer writing task)**

■ Ask the children to imagine having a ride in a micro-copter. Challenge them to list the things they might see in their playground and school. What might they see from the sky that they can't see from the ground? **(short writing task)**

■ Challenge the children to write an adventure based on a ride in a micro-copter. What device would they use to shrink to the right size in order to use the micro-copter? Where would they fly? Would they have an adventure or just enjoy the flight? Would they collect samples like the ones Ant left behind? Would they use the micro-copter to trick their friends and family? **(longer writing task)**

Other literacy activities

■ Use the six pictures on page 24 to retell the story orally. Give one sentence per picture. **(spoken language)**

Cross-curricular activities

■ In groups, act out what happens on page 8, e.g. move like Max in the mud, duck around the grass, swerve to avoid being stepped on by the dog. **(Drama)**

■ If possible, the children could find out about pond life in the local environment. **(Science)**

■ Create sound effects for the micro-copter's journey using tuned and untuned percussion instruments, emphasizing specific danger points. **(Music)**

■ Create tableaux of parts of the story, e.g. the three children looking at the fish and Ant on the other side. Photographs could be taken and speech bubbles added. The children could record the dialogue and add it to the presentation. **(Computing)**

Sam's Flood Plan
BY SIMON CHESHIRE

Curricular correlation

English National Curriculum

Spoken language	Maintain attention and participate actively in collaborative conversations, staying on topic and initiating and responding to comments
Word reading	Read words containing common suffixes
Comprehension	Make inferences on the basis of what is being said and done
	Explain and discuss their understanding of books
	Listen to, discuss and express views about stories at a level beyond that at which they can read independently

Phonics and vocabulary

GPCs	/u/ flood, up, come
Decodable 2 and 3 syllable words	anyway, upstairs, important, reports, without
Common exception words	animals, every, school, garden, door(s), because, everyone
Challenge and context words	warming, flood, house, water, listen, knew, electricity, parents, poured, sensible

Developing grammar, punctuation and spelling

Grammar and Punctuation	Subordination	They told him what to do if there was a flood. The water had been kept out – because of Sam's Flood Plan.
Spelling	The /d/ sound spelt as 'ge' at the end of words	endangered, change, page, damaged, garage

Reading assessment points (Oxford Reading Criterion Scale: Assessment Standard 3)

3. Can the children apply phonic skills and knowledge to recognize an increasing number of complex words? (READ)
7. Can the children make predictions about a text using a range of clues? (D)
9. Can the children provide simple explanations about events or information, e.g. why a character acted in a particular way? (D)
18. Can the children summarise a story, giving the main points clearly in sequence? (R)
24. Can the children confidently relate texts to their own experiences? (D)

Scottish Curriculum for Excellence

Listening and talking	I can share my thoughts about structure, characters and/or setting ENG I-19a
Reading	I am learning to select and use strategies and resources, before I read and as I read, to help make the meaning of texts clear LIT I-13a
	I can share my thoughts about structure, characters and/or setting comment on the effective choice of words and other features ENG I-19a
	I can respond to different kinds of questions and other close reading tasks and I am learning to create some questions of my own ENG I-17a

Foundation Phase Framework in Wales

Oracy	Extend their ideas or accounts by sequencing what they say and including relevant details (Speaking)
	Retell narratives or information that they have heard, sequencing events correctly (Listening)
Reading	Apply the following reading strategies with increasing independence to a range of familiar and unfamiliar texts: phonic strategies, recognition of high-frequency words, context clues, e.g. prior *knowledge*, graphic and syntactic clues, and self-correction, including re-reading and reading ahead (Reading strategies)
	Draw upon relevant personal experience and prior knowledge to support understanding of texts (Comprehension)

Northern Ireland Curriculum

Talking and Listening	Take turns at talking and listening in group and paired activities
Reading	Use a range of comprehension skills, both oral and written, to interpret and discuss texts

About this book

Sam is a boy who worries about everything, including flooding. He creates a flood plan, with instructions about what to do in a flood. When his street does flood, Sam's flood plan saves the day.

You will need

■ *Water words* Photocopy Master, *Teaching Handbook* for Year 2/P3

❯ Before reading

- ■ Look at the cover and ask the children to guess what the character is thinking and feeling. **(inferring)**
- ■ Have the children experienced a flood or seen reports of flooding on the television? **(prior knowledge)**
- ■ Ask if they can tell what the story might be about. **(predicting)**
- ■ Discuss what might cause a flood. **(activating prior knowledge)**
- ■ Ask the children to tell you any examples of water-related vocabulary that they know. This could be from prior knowledge, or your previous discussions. Look at the 'water words' in this book, e.g. *river, flood* (p.4), *poured, rain, rained* (p.10), *leaks, trickled* (p.17) and add them to the *Water words* Photocopy Master. **(developing vocabulary)**
- ■ Ask the children to predict how Sam will influence what happens in the story. **(predicting)**

> **Assessment point**
>
> Can the children make predictions about a text using a range of clues? (ORCS Standard 3, 7)

One of the things Sam worried about was the river. It ran across the field behind Sam's house. Sam was worried about the river rising and causing a flood.

He saw news reports on TV about floods. He saw streets and houses filled with muddy water. Nothing worried Sam more than that river. He worried every time it rained.

Phonic opportunity

- Draw attention to all of the words with the /u/ phoneme: *flood, up, come*. Ask the children to identify the phoneme /u/ in the words. Support children to say each phoneme and then blend the phonemes to read the word. Ask the children to think of other words with the /u/ sound.
- You may also wish to point out some of the common exception words, or practise decoding some of the challenge and context words in this book.

During reading

- Ask the children what they should do if they encounter a difficult word, modelling with an example from the book. Praise children who successfully decode unfamiliar words.
- Ask them to read to the end of the book.
- As you listen to individual children read, you might want to ask them to stop and summarize what has happened so far and predict what will happen next.
(summarizing, predicting)

Assessment point

Can the children summarise a story, giving the main points clearly in sequence?
(ORCS Standard 3, 18)

One day, during the summer, the rain fell like water poured from a bucket. It rained and rained and didn't stop for days. The river began to rise.

"Don't worry, Sam," said Mum. "The rain will stop soon."

The rain didn't stop. The river rose. Water crawled slowly across the field. It spread out towards the houses.

Sam was very worried. He gave a copy of his flood plan to every house in the street.

> After reading

Returning to the text

- Look at page 3. Describe the kitchen. What can you see through the window? Does this illustration give you a hint as to what might happen in the story? **(predicting)**

- Sam worries a lot at the start of the book. Do you worry about the same things as he does? Why does he worry when it rains? **(empathizing, personal response)** 《《《

> **Assessment point**
> Can the children confidently relate texts to their own experiences? (ORCS Standard 3, 24)

- You can see Sam's flood plan on page 7. Is this an easy plan to follow? What part of the plan could you help with? **(inferring, drawing conclusions)**

- On page 13, why does the illustrator give Sam a secret smile? **(inferring)**

- Look at the illustration of Sam on page 21 and compare it to the one on page 5. How does Sam's body language show the changes in how he is feeling? **(empathizing)** 《《《

> **Assessment point**
> Can the children provide simple explanations about events or information, e.g. why a character acted in a particular way? (ORCS Standard 3, 9)

- How did Sam face up to his worries about floods? Did his plan work? **(personal response, adopting a critical stance)**

>> *Developing comprehension*

- Go round the group, asking them to retell the story using the illustrations on pages 22 and 23. Encourage them to use water-related vocabulary. **(recall)**

⤐ *Developing vocabulary*

- On page 10, the author describes the rain falling *like water poured from a bucket*. What does the author mean? Is this a little rain or a lot of rain?
- The author writes that the water *crawled slowly across the field* (p.11). What sort of animal does the water seem to be behaving like? Does this make you feel more worried about what might happen to Sam?

⤐ *Developing grammar, punctuation and spelling*

- Look at page 6 and ask the children to identify the sentence that uses the word *if*. Discuss that this is an example of subordination. The word *if* joins a less important group of words (clause) to the main one. A subordinate clause cannot exist on its own as it is not a complete sentence. Do the same with the sentence on page 18 using the word *because*. Challenge children to identify another example of this in the book.
- Write the words *page* and *garage* on the board and ask children for the sound that they can hear in each. Discuss how the /d/ sound is sometimes spelt 'ge' at the end of words. Discuss any other examples that the children found in the text. Can they think of any other examples?

Assessment point

Can the children apply phonic skills and knowledge to recognize an increasing number of complex words?
(ORCS Standard 3, 3)

❯ Follow-up

Writing activities

- Ask the children to write instructions for Noah's flood plan. Encourage the addition of humour, e.g. *Keep the mice away from the cats!* Use computer programs to support the writing, adding illustrations and diagrams. **(short writing task)**
- Ask the children to write a picture book or use computer programs to retell and illustrate a fairy tale involving a river (e.g. *The Three Billy Goats Gruff*, to be read to younger children). **(longer writing task)**

Cross-curricular activities

- Ask parents and grandparents if the local area has ever been flooded. The information gathered could be put on a time line. **(History)**
- Create a water scene using a variety of materials and processes after studying an artist who has produced water or river scenes, e.g. Monet. **(Art and Design)**
- Create, perform and record a class composition using tuned and untuned instruments depicting a boat trip on a river (e.g. passing by a castle, under a bridge, through a tunnel, past a zoo) with the music representing the river as a recurring theme between each 'event'. **(Music)**
- Use computer programs to create a flood picture, exploring the shapes, colours and patterns of water. **(Art and Design, Computing)**

Atlantic Adventure
BY MICHAEL PERHAM AND ALEX LANE

Curricular correlation

English National Curriculum

Spoken language	Use spoken language to develop understanding through speculating, hypothesising, imagining and exploring ideas
Word reading	Continue to apply phonic knowledge and skills as the route to decode words
Comprehension	Read non-fiction books that are structured in different ways
	Answer and ask questions
	Listen to, discuss and express views about non-fiction at a level beyond that at which they can read independently

Phonics and vocabulary

GPCs	/ur/ journey, were
Decodable 2 and 3 syllable words	himself, sudden, breaking
Common exception words	more, fast, small, clothes, friends, things
Challenge and context words	Michael, world, youngest, ocean, learning, journey, route, Gibraltar, Antigua, minute, scary, break

Developing grammar, punctuation and spelling

Grammar and Punctuation	How the grammatical patterns in a sentence indicate its function as a statement, question, exclamation or command	Wow! That's so brave! (exclamation) He was only 14 years old. (statement) When was Michael born? (question) Visit Michael's website ... (command)
Spelling	The /l/ sound spelt -le at the end of words	mile, trouble, people, gentle, little, while

Reading assessment points (Oxford Reading Criterion Scale: Assessment Standard 3)

3. Can the children apply phonic skills and knowledge to recognize an increasing number of complex words? (READ)
11. Are the children beginning to use contents and index pages to locate information in non-fiction texts? (A/R)
15. Can the children read aloud with intonation, taking into account a wider range of punctuation (. ? ! ,)? (READ)
19. Are the children beginning to distinguish between fiction and non-fiction? (A)
25. Can the children talk about the features of certain non-fiction texts? (A)
26. Can the children demonstrate how to use information books? (R/A)

Scottish Curriculum for Excellence

Listening and talking	When listening and talking with others, for different purposes, I can exchange information, experiences, explanations, ideas and opinions LIT 1-09a
Reading	I am learning to select and use strategies and resources, before I read and as I read, to help make the meaning of texts clear LIT 1-13a
	Using what I know about the features of different types of texts, I can find, select, sort and use information for a specific purpose LIT 1-14a
	To help me develop an informed view, I can recognize the difference between fact and opinion LIT 1-18a

Foundation Phase Framework in Wales

Oracy	Listen to others with concentration, understanding the main points and asking for clarification if needed (Listening)
Reading	Apply the following reading strategies with increasing independence to a range of familiar and unfamiliar texts: phonic strategies, recognition of high-frequency words, context clues, e.g. *prior knowledge*, graphic and syntactic clues, and self-correction, including re-reading and reading ahead (Reading strategies)
	Identify and use text features, e.g. titles, headings and pictures, to locate and understand specific information (Reading strategy)
	Read a range of suitable texts with increasing accuracy and fluency (Reading strategies)

Northern Ireland Curriculum

Talking and Listening	Express thoughts, feelings and opinions in response to personal experiences, imaginary situations, literature, media and curricular topics and activities
Reading	Explore and begin to understand how texts are structured in a range of genres

About this book

This is a biography about Michael Perham, the youngest person to sail single-handedly across the Atlantic.

You will need

◾ *Welcome home* Photocopy Master, *Teaching Handbook* for Year 2/P3

❯ **Before reading**

◾ Ask the children what the title suggests the book might be about. Will it be fiction or non-fiction? What evidence do the children have for their opinions? **(deducing, inferring)** ≪ ≪ ≪

Assessment point

Are the children beginning to distinguish between fiction and non-fiction?
(ORCS Standard 3, 19)

◾ Look at the contents page and then at pages 2 and 3. Encourage the children to find the micro-friends and read their speech bubbles. Why does Cat think Michael is brave? **(inferring)**

◾ Looking back at the contents page, ask the children which chapters they would be most interested in reading. As they go on to look at those sections, ask them to think about the comments made by Cat and Tiger (as fully as they can). **(personal response)** ≪ ≪ ≪

Assessment point

Are the children beginning to use contents and index pages to locate information in non-fiction texts?
(ORCS Standard 3, 11)

❯ *Phonic opportunity*

◾ Draw attention to all of the words with the /ur/ phoneme: *journey, were.* Ask children to identify the phoneme /ur/ in the words. Support children to say each phoneme and then blend the phonemes to read the word. Ask the children to think of other words with the /ur/ sound.

◾ You may also wish to point out some of the common exception words, or practise decoding some of the challenge and context words in this book.

- Scan the text for words in bold and show the children how to use the glossary at the back of the book. **(developing vocabulary)**
- Why is the font for Michael's blog different from the main text (e.g. p.3)? **(previewing the text)**

During reading

- Ask the children what they should do if they encounter a difficult word, modelling with an example from the book. Praise children who successfully decode unfamiliar words.

《《《

> **Assessment point**
>
> Can the children apply phonic skills and knowledge to recognize an increasing number of complex words? (ORCS Standard 3, 3)

- Ask them to read to the end of page 7. Then look at pages 8 and 9 together, with a globe if possible, and discuss the route of Michael's journey. **(visualizing)**
- Ask them to choose a section from the contents page which appeals to them. (They may have time to read more than one, depending on the child.)

After reading

Returning to the text

- Ask each child to tell the group which section they chose to read, why they chose it, and one interesting piece of information they discovered from their reading. **(recalling)**
- As you discuss each chosen section, ask the children how these pages differ from a story page (layout, information boxes, maps, photographs, glossary words in bold).

《《《《

> **Assessment point**
>
> Can the children talk about the features of certain non-fiction texts? (ORCS Standard 3, 25)

Developing comprehension

- Working in pairs, ask the children to think of questions to ask the rest of the group. **(questioning)**
- Looking at pages 10 and 11, ask them to list the most important things Michael had to take with him. **(determining importance)**

Developing vocabulary

- Model the process of looking up a word in the glossary. Ask the children to return to the spread they selected and decide if any of the words not already in the glossary need explaining. If they do, work in pairs to compose glossary entries, using class dictionaries.

- Check that they understand the purpose of the index. Are there any other words that they would like to be in the index?

Assessment point
Can the children demonstrate how to use information books? (ORCS Standard 3, 26)

What to see at sea

You might think that there is nothing to look at at sea. But Michael saw lots of things ...

Extract from Michael's blog: 4th December, 2006

Had a fantastic display of dolphins before sunset. They must have been with the boat for at least 2 hours. They were jumping up in the air and being crazy. One dolphin made a huge jump out of the top of a wave. It was amazing.

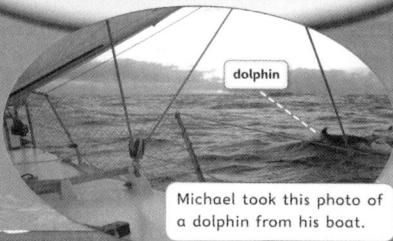

Extract from Michael's blog: 16th December, 2006

Another flying fish jumped into the **cockpit** today. My dad said he saw a great long shark following him when we were drifting around. It was about 4 metres long! Scary stuff. I'm glad that didn't jump into my cockpit!

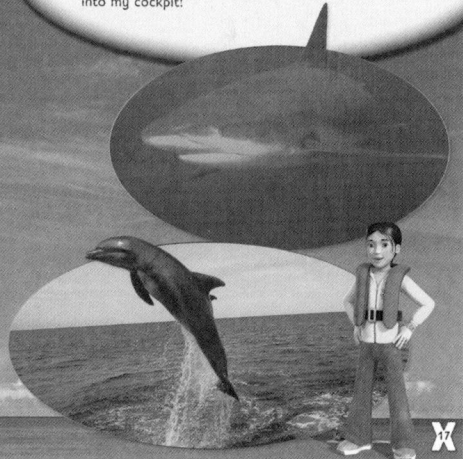

dolphin

Michael took this photo of a dolphin from his boat.

Developing grammar, punctuation and spelling

- Turn to pages 2 and 5 and ask the children to identify a statement, exclamation and question on these pages. Now turn to page 23 and ask them to identify a command. Discuss the punctuation that is used for each and the words that help indicate the sentence type. Give each child a double-page spread of their own to look at and identify the types of sentence on each. Give time for each child to explain their conclusions to the rest of the group.
- Write the words *mile* and *people* on the board and ask children for the sound that they can hear in each. Discuss how the /l/ sound is sometimes spelt 'le' at the end of words. Can they think of any other examples?

Developing fluency

- Ask the children to find the extracts from Michael's blog throughout the book. Working in pairs, ask them to speak each section, concentrating on highlighting Michael's excitement.

Assessment point

Can the children read aloud with intonation, taking into account a wider range of punctuation (. ? ! ,)? (ORCS Standard 3, 15)

Record breaking!

On 3rd January 2007, Michael Perham broke a world record!
He became the youngest person to sail across the Atlantic Ocean by himself.
He was only 14 years old.
It took him just over 6 weeks. He sailed more than 4700 miles.

What a long way.

North Atlantic Ocean

Start

Finish

Wow! That's so brave!

South Atlantic Ocean

Michael on his boat.

> Follow-up

Writing activities

- Ask the children to design a welcome home poster for Michael, using the *Welcome home* Photocopy Master. Encourage them to use the vocabulary which Michael himself used in his blog. **(short writing task)**

- Ask them to imagine that they are going to take a sea journey. They should write a diary or a blog of their adventures. As this is a story and not factual, there could be encounters with anyone, e.g. fantastic creatures or pirates. They could use computer programs to write their story, adding illustrations and sound effects. **(longer writing task)**

Cross-curricular activities

- The children could create a 3D display of sailing boats. **(Art and Design)**

- The children could discuss how Michael could raise funds for his round-the-world trip and check his website. **(Computing, PHSE)**

- They could listen to some music depicting the sea, e.g. Fingal's Cave, Scherezade, and then compose their own sea music (calm and stormy). They could record the musical ideas using invented signs and symbols, and rehearse and perform the compositions. **(Music)**

- They could create a sea scene using a variety of materials and processes after studying an artist who has produced seascapes. **(Art and Design)**

- They could use computer programs to design a sailing boat. **(Computing, DT, Maths)**

The Water Cycle

BY STEVE PARKER

Curricular correlation

English National Curriculum

Spoken language	Participate in discussions and debates
Word reading	Read accurately by blending the sounds in words that contain the graphemes taught so far, especially recognising alternative sounds for graphemes
Comprehension	Read non-fiction books that are structured in different ways
	Discuss the sequence of events in books and how items of information are related
	Answer and ask questions

Phonics and vocabulary

GPCs	/ai/ rain, day, make, they
Decodable 2 and 3 syllable words	hillside, eventually, rainwater, treatment, toothpaste, otherwise
Common exception words	water, fast, animals, every, cold, friends, sea, grow
Challenge and context words	bounced, water, worms, gentle, pours, chemicals, ice, wheels, wires, Earth, vapour

Developing grammar, punctuation and spelling

Grammar and Punctuation	Commas to separate items in a list	The soap, dirt, toothpaste and other substances
Spelling	The /or/ sound spelt 'a' before 'l' or 'll'	all, fall, animals, tall, chemicals, small, also, called, wall

Reading assessment points (Oxford Reading Criterion Scale: Assessment Standard 3)

3.	Can the children apply phonic skills and knowledge to recognize an increasing number of complex words? (READ)
7.	Can the children make predictions about a text using a range of clues? (D)
9.	Can the children provide simple explanations about events or information? (D)
15.	Can the children read aloud with intonation, talking into account a wider range of punctuation (. ? ! ,)? (READ)
20.	Having read a text, can the children find the answers to questions, both written and oral? (R)

Scottish Curriculum for Excellence

Listening and talking	I can exchange information, experiences, explanations, ideas and opinions, and clarify points by asking questions or by asking others to say more LIT 1-09a
Reading	I can use my knowledge of sight vocabulary, phonics, context clues, punctuation and grammar to read with understanding and expression (ENG 1-12a)
	Using what I know about the features of different types of texts, I can find, select, sort and use information for a specific purpose LIT 1-14a
	To show my understanding across different areas of learning, I can identify and consider the purpose and main ideas of a text LIT 1-16a

Foundation Phase Framework in Wales

Oracy	Contribute to discussion, keeping a focus on the topic and taking turns to speak (Collaboration and discussion)
Reading	Apply the following reading strategies with increasing independence to a range of familiar and unfamiliar texts: phonic strategies, recognition of high-frequency words, context clues, e.g. *prior knowledge*, graphic and syntactic clues, and self-correction, including re-reading and reading ahead (Reading strategies)
	Make links between texts read and new information about the topic (Response and analysis)

Northern Ireland Curriculum

Talking and Listening	Present ideas and information with some structure and sequence
Reading	Read, explore, understand and make use of a range of traditional and digital texts

About this book This book follows a raindrop character through the water cycle.	**You will need** ■ *The journey of a water droplet* Photocopy Master, *Teaching Handbook* for Year 2/P3

❯ Before reading

■ Look at the front cover. What do the children think a book with this title will be about? Look at the contents page. Were they right? Ask them to predict what each spread might be about. Which sections might give information or ideas that are new to them? **(previewing the text, predicting)** ⟪⟪⟪

Assessment point

Can the children make predictions about a text using a range of clues? (ORCS Standard 3, 7)

■ Working in pairs, ask the children to choose one section title. Discuss what they think it will be about. Then read the spread to confirm or amend predictions. Take feedback from around the group. **(predicting)**

■ Find the index together. Select one entry and check where the reference leads. **(engaging readers)**

■ Turn to the glossary. Ask the children to recap the purpose of a glossary and to compare it to the purpose of the contents page and index. Ask them to browse the book to find the words in bold that indicate a glossary entry. How do the explanations help them to understand the text more easily? **(activating prior knowledge)**

❯ *Phonic opportunity*

■ Draw attention to all of the words with the /ai/ phoneme: *rain, day, make, they*. Ask the children to identify the phoneme /ai/ in the words. Support children to say each phoneme and then blend the phonemes to read the word. Ask the children to think of other words with the /ai/ sound.

■ You may also wish to point out some of the common exception words, or practise decoding some of the challenge and context words in this book.

■ Read pages 2 and 3 together. What do the children think will be the role and purpose of the water droplet? Read the next two spreads together. Then ask them to read on to page 13. Ask them to tell the group about a new idea or fact that that they have learnt. **(predicting, recall)**

> During reading

■ Ask the children to read the rest of the book and find another new fact to share with the group when they have finished reading.

■ Remind them what they should do if they encounter a difficult word, modelling with an example from the book. Praise children who can successfully decode unfamiliar words.

Assessment point

Can the children apply phonic skills and knowledge to recognize an increasing number of complex words? (ORCS Standard 3, 3)

■ Encourage them to check the glossary entries as they read.

> After reading

Returning to the text

■ The children should present their newly-found facts to the rest of the group and be prepared to answer questions. **(recalling, questioning)**

Assessment point

Having read a text, can the children find the answers to questions, both written and oral? (ORCS Standard 3, 20)

■ Ask each child to prepare one question from their favourite section to ask the group. **(recalling, questioning)**

■ As you discuss each chosen section, ask the children how the illustrations help the reader to understand the text. Which was the most interesting/informative photograph or illustration and why? **(personal response, adopting a critical stance, visualizing)**

Developing comprehension

- Ask the children to work in pairs to decide which was:
  - ☐ the most interesting place for the water droplet to be.
  - ☐ the most useful place to be.
  - ☐ the most unpleasant place to be.

  Remind them to use the contents page and index to help them make their decisions. **(determining importance, empathizing)**

- 'Hot-seat' the water droplet. The children could take it in turns to answer questions about the water cycle in role as the water droplet. **(recalling, empathizing)**

Assessment point

Can the children provide simple explanations about events or information?
(ORCS Standard 3, 9)

Ice-cold water

It's now winter. The water is so cold, it cannot flow. It becomes hard and solid. This is called freezing. Frozen water is called ice. A sheet of ice freezes on the surface of the water.

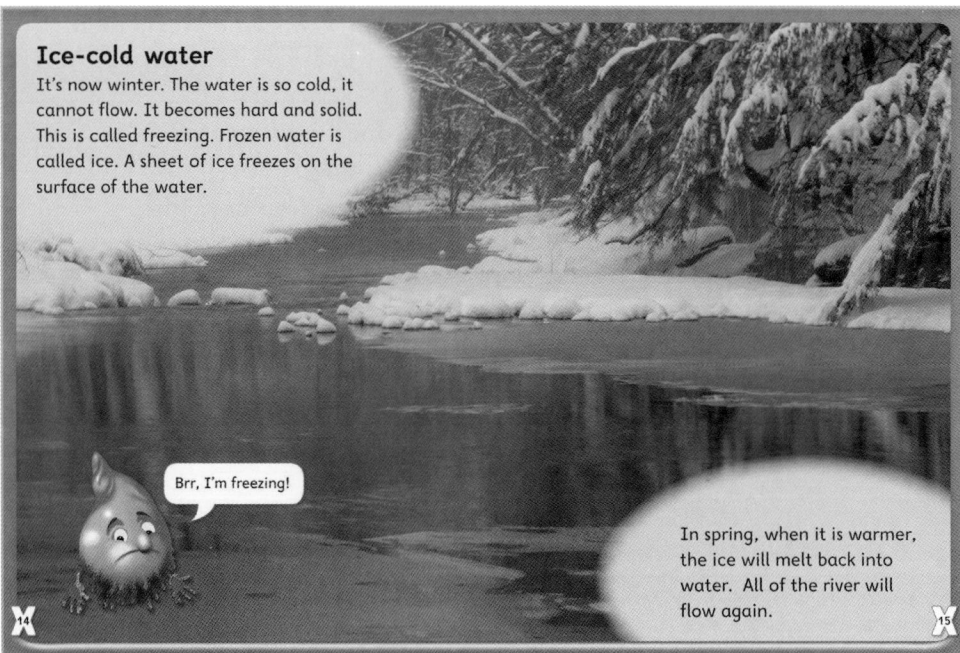

Brr, I'm freezing!

In spring, when it is warmer, the ice will melt back into water. All of the river will flow again.

⤳ Developing grammar, punctuation and spelling

- ▦ Write the sentence *The soap, dirt, toothpaste and other substances are taken out* on the board. Can the children identify the punctuation mark that appears twice here? Discuss that it is a comma and it can be used to separate things in a list.
- ▦ Write the words *wall* and *called* on the board and ask children for the sound that they can hear in each. Discuss how the /or/ sound is spelt with an 'a' when it comes before 'l' or 'll'. Look at the examples the children found in the text. Can they think of any other examples?

⤳ Developing fluency

- ▦ Demonstrate how to read pages 2–5 with appropriate pace and expression. Ask the children to read aloud round the group in pairs, a paragraph at a time. ⟪⟪⟪

Assessment point

Can the children read aloud with intonation, talking into account a wider range of punctuation (. ? ! ,)? (ORCS Standard 3, 15)

> **Follow-up**

Writing activities

- Make a list of all the ways we use water at home and school. Use pages 10 and 11 to help. **(longer writing task)**

- Design a poster to show how we could save water in the home. **(short writing task)**

Cross-curricular activities

- Dramatize parts of the journey of the water droplet. **(Drama)**

- After a class discussion, draw a plan of the journey of the water droplet in groups using the *The journey of a water droplet* Photocopy Master (i.e. raindrop, dinosaur, soil, stream etc.) **(Science, Geography)**

- Make a 'Wonderful Water' presentation. Show all the activities you can do which rely on water in all its various forms, e.g. skiing in snow, playing at the beach, ice hockey, making a cup of tea. Use computer programs to add photographs and sound. **(Computing)**

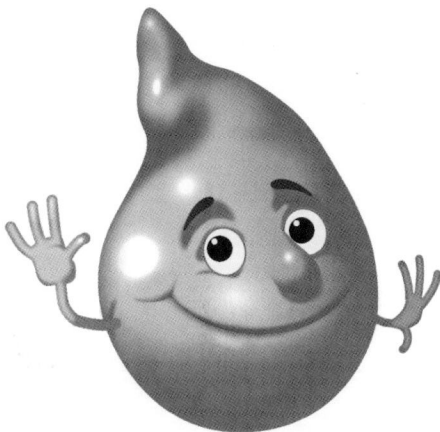